In loving memory of my earthly fathers, Deacon Charles Thomas Wilcox and Willie Edward Lashley, Jr.

In honor of my mother, Deaconess Alice Hunt Wilcox; my godmother, Georgette Brown Kimball; my spiritual father, Bishop Shelton C. Daniel, founder and senior pastor, Greater Joy Missionary Baptist Church, Rocky Mount and Roanoke Rapids, North Carolina; and everyone who has ever had a pit experience.

As you read my testimony, it is my prayer that you will be encouraged.

Acknowledgments

Special thanks to Mrs. Alice Wilcox, my mother; Georgette Brown Kimball, my "God" mother; Bishop Shelton Daniel, pastor and friend; and my five sisters, *Arnetta, Phyllis, Tamatha, Alicia, and Charletta.*

Thanks also to my prayer team, *you know who you are;* "Team Tonia"; and my spiritual brothers, *Victor Fenner, Philip "King" Rountree, Mark Barfield, Teicher Patterson, Donald Boyd, Thurman Lee, and Retired Air Force MSGT Larry L. Copeland*

Remember

Even though you planned evil against me, God planned good to come out of it. This was to keep many people alive, as he is doing now. Genesis 50:20 (God's Word Translation)

No one looked on you with pity or had compassion enough to do any of these things for you. Rather, you were thrown out into the open field, for on the day you were born you were despised. (Ezekiel 16:5, NIV)

No one had the slightest interest in you; no one pitied you or cared for you. On that day when you were born, you were dumped out into a field and left to die, unwanted. (Ezekiel 16:5, The Living Bible)

No one who saw you felt sorry enough for you to do any of these things. But you were thrown into an open field. You were rejected when you were born. (Ezekiel 16:5, God's Word Translation)

It is so, in Jesus's name. Amen!

PART I

Faith

Jesus on Faith

I can do all things through Christ which strengtheneth me. (Philippians 4:13)

He staggered not at the promise of God through unbelief; but was strong in faith, giving glory to God;

And being fully persuaded that, what he had promised, he was able also to perform.

And therefore it was imputed to him for righteousness. (Romans 4:20–22)

But they that wait upon the Lord shall renew their strength; they shall mount up with wings as eagles; they shall run, and not be weary; and they shall walk, and not faint. (Isaiah 40:31)

A man's heart deviseth his way: but the Lord directeth his steps. (Proverbs 16:9)

The fear of man bringeth a snare: but whoso putteth his trust in the Lord shall be safe. (Proverbs 29:25)

For with God nothing shall be impossible. (Luke 1:37)

O Lord my God, I cried unto thee, and thou hast healed me. (Psalm 30:2)

And God shall wipe away all tears from their eyes; and there shall be no more death, neither sorrow, nor crying, neither shall there be any more pain: for the former things are passed away. (Revelations 21:4)

Introduction

In life, we find ourselves in different situations, some by force, others by choice. Regardless to the circumstances surrounding our situations, we can all relate to this one thing: *"life happens, but God reigns."*

Over the years, I have had the privilege of reading "self-help" books written by *best-known authors such as Bishop T. D. Jakes, Dr. Jamal Bryant, Prophetess Juanita Bynum,* and *Iyanla Vanzant,* all great authors and ministers in their own right.

But as life happened, I found myself reading and studying the word of God more and more each time. I must confess that even though I love the books written by these authors, it was God and his word that sustained me through my test and trials.

With this being said, as I journeyed through the details that prompted the writing of this book, I felt the Holy Spirit telling me to share. Share how you can win the battle without fighting the war. In other words, share real-life experiences and how the application of God's word makes the difference.

Revelation 12:11 states, "And they overcame him by the blood of the Lamb, and by the word of their *testimony*; and they loved not their lives unto the death." A testimony is simply a public recounting of a religious experience. In other words, your "test" shall become your "testimony."

It is with humility and thankfulness that you have given me the opportunity to share my "testimony" with you. *From the Pit to the Palace: A Testimony of Faith, Forgiveness, and Freedom* is not a typical "self-help" book with seven principles to apply and life changes. Instead, *From the Pit to the Palace: A Testimony of Faith, Forgiveness, and Freedom* is a true story based on intimate events of my life.

So, as I let you into my life, please note all accounts are tested, tried, and proven true. "God is not a man, that he should lie; neither the son of man, that he should repent: hath he said, and shall he not do it? or hath he spoken, and shall he not make it good?" (*Numbers 23:19*).

It is my prayer that you will receive and understand that a pit is not always a physical dwelling. It is not always a place where someone has placed you. Your pit can be anything from mental distress to physical misery. Only you can identify your pit, and I pray that by the time you finish reading my story, you will have done just that.

Once you recognize, identify, and accept your pit experience, petition God for clear direction and begin to trust him for provision and watch him make a way.

Welcome to my life, welcome to my story. It is a great place to be! To God be the glory for the wonderful things he has done for me!

> And we know that all things work together
> for good to them that love God, to them who are
> the called according to his purpose. (*Romans 8:28*)

A special message to my nieces and nephews:

I pray that I have been a positive example to you thus far. I pray God will use each of you mightily that one day you will tell your story. I am praying abundant blessings over each of you and your personal ministries. I love you all!

Nieces: Morgan, Dominique, Kyndahl, Cierra, Faith, Errin, Destiny, and McKenzie

Nephews: Ryan, Malik, Tarik, Tyler, Jeremy, Demetry, Morrell, Cassius, and Jaquan

Number one great nephew: Brantley Bulluck

Like many young African Americans who are exposed to situations in life, I agree they do have an influence that we later credit for the person we turn out to be or not to be. Coming from a single mother home with four siblings at the time of my rebirth, most people thought my sisters and I would not "amount to anything" *but God!*

God saw it necessary to bless my mother and the fruit of her womb. In 1973, my mother not only married the love of her life, but my sisters and I later learned that he would also become the love of our lives. Like all teenagers who clearly don't understand the plan God has for us, when we are conceived in our mother's womb, I had a hard time accepting this man as my father. But God in his infinite wisdom knew the day would come when all things would be reconciled, lessons would be taught and learned, and "our" love would be called home to be the angel that watches over us now.

Deacon Charles Thomas Wilcox
"Buck"
March 20, 1949–December 18, 2014

This story of being able to love when the situation seems too hard to love is the beginning of the lesson and the blessing of *From the Pit to the Palace: A Story of Faith, Forgiveness, and Freedom*. As time progressed, many displays of God's love were apparent all around me. For example, my father (Buck) had sons of his own when he met my mother. Between the two of them and over time, our family grew exponentially. Eight years later, I went from having four sisters to now having five sisters and two brothers. But God made a way.

Faith assures us of things we expect and convinces us of the existence of things we cannot see *(Hebrews 11:1, God's Word Translation)*. Therefore, it is imperative as a child to be in right relationship with your parents *(Matthew 19:19)*, and parents should be in right relationship with God *(Proverbs 22:6)*. This is not always apparent in the life of a strong willed child.

However, the sooner this lesson is learned, the sooner things will begin to prosper in your life. No, it is never easy to accept those things in life that cause us hurt and disappointment, but God knows it takes those experiences to create in us that clean heart that is mentioned in *Psalm 51:10*. Resting on this word from the Almighty God gives renewed strength to continue the journey.

There is no better feeling than knowing when a request is made *(Psalm 51:9–11)*. God in his magnificent glory will honor that request when it comes from a pure and clean heart. Now, it is important to know that this clean heart did not happen to me all at once.

Cleaning is a process, and it is a process that does not happen immediately. For example, when you start a cleaning project, no matter what it may be, you will get tired. You will have to stop and catch your breath, drink a glass of water, say a prayer, or whatever you do to regain strength for the task. The same holds true when it comes to perfecting a clean heart. There will be times when you become so exhausted that you just have to step back, reach up, and be confident of this very thing that he which hath begun a good work in you will perform it until the day of Jesus Christ *(Philippians 1:6)*.

What more can we ask for when we live in a world where there is so much chaos and confusion, so much hurt and pain. But knowing that we serve a God who has promised the harvest will be good, if we faint not *(Isaiah 40:31)*, gives enough assurance to keep pushing even when your strength is gone. It is at this time the strength of God is made manifest in your life and he begins to do exceedingly and abundantly above all we can ask or think. "Now unto him that is able to do exceeding abundantly above all that we ask or think, according to the power that worketh in us" *(Ephesians 3:20)*.

Faith can be a real challenge, one of life's most challenging challenges. It can be the deciding factor between life and death. However, without faith, it is impossible to please God *(Hebrews 11:6)*. As a child who felt angry, upset, and frustrated for a long time, it was truly difficult to embrace faith, or so I thought.

I accepted the call of Christ on my life and was baptized at the age of nine. I honestly did not fully understand what was happening, but I knew that it was different. I knew that something was waiting on me; therefore, I had to get to a place where I was OK with being different. Someone reading this book just received the answer to the question they always wanted to ask. "Why is she like that?" or maybe you wanted to ask, "What's wrong with her?" At this point, I do not believe the answers are relevant. What I do believe though is that this message of *faith, forgiveness, and freedom* sheds light on why many Christians, like myself, are seen as "different."

The word of God reminds us in *Exodus 19:5*: "Now therefore, if ye will obey my voice indeed, and keep my covenant, then ye shall be a *peculiar* treasure unto me above all people: for all the earth is mine."

Although it seems like it sometimes, peculiarity is not a curse. In fact, it is a distinguishing characteristic. One that is different from the norm. In other words, an individual who possesses the peculiar trait is one who doesn't mind being alone; for it is during the alone time when he or she executes a level of faith that truly does surpass human understanding.

This faith is what I most often times refer to as "stupid" faith. Looking through your carnal (natural) eyes, it seems to be unintelligent and unreasonable. However, through spiritual eyes, it is the epitome of an imagination gone wild. In other words, it is being able to step out on nothing knowing that God is able to turn it into something.

This faith I am talking about is an action that requires you to be in agreement with God's word. It is more than acknowledging that God is who he says he is, but it requires us to believe that God can do what he says he can do, for to believe is to accept God and his infinite wisdom as truth.

Let me be clear, there are some prerequisites to being able to apply "stupid" faith. When I reflect on my life and the basis of this testimonial, I can see clearly why it took more than just saying that I believe what God says. It took being able to stare straight down the nose of adversity and make a promise to Satan that he would not and, I repeat, would not get any of God's glory for the trials I had been through. For me, this meant being able to get up on days when all I really wanted to do was stay in the bed with the covers over my head and not talk to anyone. Not even to God.

I know this sounds crazy for someone who has never been in this position. But for those of us who have been so discouraged with life and so frustrated by its challenges, this is real. To just wake up becomes a task, and then you tell me to get up, dress up, and show up. My initial thought was, "Oh my God, you must be crazy!"

During this time, I was getting up, dressing up, and showing up in a workplace that was truly not Tonia friendly. Every cheek I turned was slapped by someone. I faced a direct attack on my character that took "stupid" faith to shame the devil and please the Lord. I began to think that God was an upscale version of Steve Harvey. What do I mean by that, you may ask? In my mind, God was a comedian, and I happened to be the joke of the day.

Please don't attempt to analyze that too deeply for I know God has a sense of humor, but I also know that God doesn't allow us to go through any more than with him we can't handle. Take a minute to reflect on *Philippians 4:13*, "I can do all things through Christ which strengtheneth me."

This attack on my character included very harsh words such as sabotage, harass, single out, and, yes, sleeping with the "enemy" to get what I had obtained. Now, if there is anyone who may be thinking well, did you? The answer to your question is unequivocally no. Remember, I serve a God who owns the cattle on a thousand hills. Therefore, it is not necessary nor has it ever been necessary for me to jeopardize my father's seed and sell my soul to the devil. We have not, because we ask not!

Asking requires *faith*. The kind of faith that says, if I ask, I will receive *(Matthew 7:7)*, even if I'm asking a God that I don't physically see every day. For many, it is a need to be able to see who we are asking and what we are asking for, but for a child who knows her father can provide, has always provided, and will continue to provide, seeing is not necessary, for we truly shall receive if we can only believe.

Faith is not a curse. Instead, it is a key that unlocks the door to things that seem impossible. *Faith* is the solid presence of expectation that a particular thing will come to fruition in your life. It is the spiritually visible sign that indicates the word of God is true. Let's be clear, faith is not a feeling; it cannot be seen through natural eyes. You can't taste it, you can't feel it, and you certainly can't smell. *Faith* is that one thing that you know, and no one can convince you otherwise. In other words, *faith* is hearing what God said, knowing what God said, and believing what God said. Do you know what you heard, do you know who said it, and do you believe what was said? If so, that's faith. Now may I ask, where is your faith?

As I reflect on the many events in my life when I had to execute my "stupid" faith, I will intentionally select the most recent event. Let me warn you, the details of this event will be mind-boggling. As you read through the events that prompted me to pen this story to paper, I am certain you will have many questions. But I promise you, if you continue to read through to the end, your questions will be answered, your faith will be increased, and your strength will be renewed. The facts of this situation are not altered in any form. They are true and can be verified and confirmed. This is a real story of hate, envy, deceit, and the list goes on.

The journey began in August of 2000. I was hired by one of the local school agencies. I spent almost nine years as the administrative assistant/receptionist/bookkeeper. To be honest, these were the best served years spent with this organization. I know for some people this position is not one that brings exceptional glory, but for me, it brought satisfaction at the end of each day. I was happy to serve a community where there was so much love, one where people looked out for each other and one where the employees at the school seemed much like family.

During these nine years, I had several principals as my immediate supervisors. However, I attribute much of my success and knowledge on my first principal. This is the lady who saw value in me and gave me the opportunity to serve the school. She made sure I had a clear understanding of many of the processes that made a school run smoothly. At the time, I honestly was not interested in learning any more than I needed to. My only concern was to get through the days and weeks, get home safely, receive my paycheck, and buy more shoes. In my mind, all of that "other stuff" was not needed, not necessary, and certainly not wanted. Little did I know that all of this "other stuff" where footprints in the sand where my steps were being ordered by the Lord. "The steps of a good man are ordered by the Lord: and he delighteth in his way" *(Psalms 37:23)*.

At this time in my life, I had so much emotional baggage that being confused seemed like a compliment. Yes, I was unable to think clearly. While I was able to function and complete day-to-day tasks, I honestly did not possess the qualities needed to make rational decisions. I was unaware at the time that the enemy had stolen from me the very thing that God wanted to use in me. He (the enemy) had attacked my mind and taken away my desire to learn and the value I added. Therefore, he (God) used this principal to be firm with me and insist that I apply my God-given knowledge. Today, I am so happy to know that God was delighted enough with me that he ordered my steps.

As time progressed, many other leaders were assigned to lead the school, but for some reason, I was the only constant. Each one brought their own unique style of leading, and each one taught me valuable lessons. Looking back, I can see that entire experience was crafted by God to increase my strength for the journey that waited ahead. Hear me when I tell you this, the God I serve will never allow you to be in a situation that you are ill equipped for. It may seem like it at the time, but have faith and believe he will see you through.

Nine years not only brought satisfaction from serving, but it created beautiful friendships, and I am happy to say many of those friendships live on today. Though we saw the school permanently close, retirements, death, new seasons, marriages, some people move away, promotions, and many other wonderful events that occur in our lives, there was no event more meaningful than the day I met my spiritual father, Bishop Shelton C. Daniel.

As I stated I was the administrative assistant at a middle school, and the middle school sat in the heart of a family community, a community where everyone was related. Therefore every event had an impact on everyone around. One day, I was working, and someone's child (I have tried for many years to remember this child's name, but I can't) came into the front office. This child and I were having a conversation about church.

The child called me out and said, "You are always talking about church. I have never seen you at my church."

While many of you probably would have thought that was inappropriate for this child to say, I found it fascinating. At least he/she was listening to what I said. Time went on, and I began to really think about what he/she said. As adults, we need to take the time to hear from a child for the Bible tell us *(Isaiah 11:6c)*, and a little child shall lead them. Boy, am I happy I was led by a child.

I began to attend services at the family-oriented community church. Bishop Daniel, then Rev. Daniel, was the pastor. Our paths crossed, and I had no idea what was going to happen next.

Active in the lives of the youth in the church, Bishop Daniel made many appearances at the school. His love for children made him one of the most welcoming sites on the campus. As God would have it one day, Bishop Daniel and I had a conversation, and he too invited me to worship with him and his congregation. I finally garnered up enough nerve to attend the service once, attend the service again and again and again, and finally it happened.

Bishop Daniel preached a sermon entitled "I'm Making A Comeback!" Like always, at the end of the sermon, Bishop extended a call to those who did not have a relationship with Christ, who had strayed away from Christ, or who just wanted to be a part of his ministry. Before I knew it, I had made my way to the altar where he was standing, and he began to pray. I honestly can't tell you what call I thought I was answering at that particular time, but in hindsight, I can tell you all three appeals were very fitting for my life.

I know, quit thinking what you are thinking. Yes, I was saved, got saved when I was nine years old. At the time I joined Bishop Daniel's ministry, I had been saved and actively showing up for service for twenty-eight years. I served on many ministries and even lead a few. I knew God, or so I thought.

What I did not know was once again, I was unaware at the time that the enemy had stolen from me the very thing that God wanted to use in me. He (the enemy) had attacked my mind and taken away my desire to learn and the value I added. Therefore, he (God) used this man of God, Bishop Daniel, to be firm with me and insist that I apply my God-given knowledge. Today, I am so happy to know that God was delighted enough with me that he ordered my steps. "The steps of a good man are ordered by the Lord: and he delighteth in his way" *(Psalms 37:23).*

When I finally had an opportunity to have a conversation with Bishop Daniel, he told me, "I knew you were struggling from the first time we met. I began praying for you then."

To God be the glory for a man who has unselfishly extended himself to me in so many ways. He has invested and poured so much into my life that had I not humbled myself at the request of a child, I would probably not be here to bless you today.

What does this have to do with faith, you may ask? It takes faith to step out on nothing and believe that something is there. While you may be thinking that it was my faith that got me to that place, please stand corrected. It was nothing that I did or could have done on my own to get there. Remember, my only concern was to get through the days and weeks, get home safely, receive my paycheck, and buy more shoes.

OK now, stop shaking your head. If it wasn't for the faith of others, many of you would not be where you are today. I am glad they looked at nothing through natural eyes and allowed God to help them see something through spiritual eyes. It is because of this, I stand flat foot and firm today knowing without a doubt.

Fast-Forwarding to 2009

Like many other business entities, the school district was succumbed to economic challenges. This being said, three schools were closed. As fate would have it, the school I was assigned to was on the closure list. Once again, "the steps of a good man are ordered by the Lord: and he delighteth in his way" *(Psalms 37:23)*. My new assignment was now coordinator of student information at the district office.

Let me warn you, please don't read too fast. If you notice, I said, "my new *assignment* (not job) was now coordinator of student information at the district office." I must admit, it was nice to know that once again someone saw value in me and decided my skills were much needed upon his retirement. The word of God says, "A man's *gift* maketh room for him, and bringeth him before great men" *(Proverbs 18:16)*.

Little did I know that this assignment was going to be the start of a journey that would have many highs and lows in both my professional and personal life. Before I start to pen anything about this time in my life, I must acknowledge the coordinator whose position I was assigned upon his retirement in 2009. He too made sure I had a clear understanding of what was needed to make the district run smoothly. For those who may not know, student information is the funding source for school districts, and it was all entrusted in my hands. Thank you *CTA* for acknowledging my skills and talent.

Even as I pen the words to this paper, I can clearly see my steps were being ordered again. In my mind, it seems unfortunate not to see what God is doing, while he's doing it. However, I can only imagine if we knew all that was happening in the spiritual realm, how would we react. To be honest, when I look back over the past eight, years there were many opportunities to give out, give in, and give up. How beautiful it is when we recognize and acknowledge that our steps have been and continue to be ordered by the Lord *(Psalms 37:23)*.

First and foremost, my assignment exposed some people for who they really are. For the sake of simplicity, I will say, you really learn a lot about someone's personality when you have been called from among them to serve in a different capacity. As long as I was an administrative assistant, everything and everybody were good. But as soon as God opened a door for me to pursue a college degree, the cards began to stack up against me.

The enemy went on immediate attack. In 2009, the pastor of the church I had become fond of was summoned by God to do work in another city. I guess you are probably wondering what this had to do with me. Well, I am glad you gave me the opportunity to expound further. Not only was he my spiritual father, we had become good friends. And at this time in my life, all I was used to was friends walking off and leaving me alone.

Please, don't judge me for that last statement. My experience to this point with "friends" was that of a spiritual leader who explicitly told me my only issue was the devil had gotten a hold of me; a boyfriend of five years who decided I was no longer what he wanted or needed in his life; a girlfriend who thought it funny and, yes, laughed in my face because she had details of the ex-boyfriend's "new" friend that I was not aware of; a serious health scare; three surgeries; the school was closed by the district; unsure of a new job assignment; crazy car issues seemingly every week; and living with my sister and her family.

To sum this up in one statement, I was spiritually dead, mentally exhausted, emotionally drained, and financially broke. And now this. I became very angry. Angry at the fact this man was about to walk out on me too. Where would I go for fellowship? What would happen to me now? I was not about to drive forty-five minutes just to hear him preach. That just did not seem necessary, when I could catch Bishop T. D. Jakes every Sunday and not even get dressed.

Unfortunately for me, I was so blinded by hurt I could not see that God was simultaneously ordering our steps and that I would later become an integral part of his ministry. I must also add, not only did I drive forty-five minutes one way to be under his teaching, but I did it faithfully for the 8:00 a.m. service. This is where I found the anointing was fresh and the word was more powerful. This does not minimize any of his messages, because with God, they have all been powerful. *Note the unknown steps that were being ordered for my growth and this project.*

I was finally starting to feel like I was coming back to life, when once again, the devil was standing around the corner waiting on me. After sitting under the teachings of Bishop Daniel, I realized I was my biggest deterrent to my breakthrough. I know that's hard for some people to digest, but yes, many of us are our own biggest enemy. Especially when you always think everything wrong is because of someone else.

In my tenure as student information coordinator for the school district, I served humbly. Day one of this assignment, I knew I was going to have to rely on God for the strength and tenacity I was going to need if I was going to be successful. It was obvious my very presence made the devil mad. For those of you who may be saying, "She ain't all that," I beg to differ, and here is why.

With this assignment, I was the youngest in an administrative role in the building. I had the largest office. Yeah, you know the one. The corner office where there is a window, minimal traffic, it was quiet and inviting. I made everyone who entered into my space feel as though they were home sitting on their sofa. There was soft music, drinks, snacks, books (Fruit of the Spirit), and a welcoming spirit. Believe me, as time progressed, my office became the place of "refuge" as was noted by all who stopped by.

In hindsight, I see this assignment as one far greater than managing student information. It was here that I was allowed to pour into the lives of so many people who were hurting. The one thing I learned was when you place your mind on caring for someone else, God will place his hands on caring for you. Many times I prayed with and for others, I listened when someone needed to talk, I wiped many tears and kept lots of secrets. I sowed seeds of peace even in the midst of discord. Why, you might ask. Simply because I know that God is not the author of confusion, but *of* peace *(1 Corinthians 14:33)* but more so because I had had enough chaos in my own life that I was ready to reap a harvest of peace. "Be not deceived; God is not mocked: for whatsoever a man soweth, that shall he also reap" *(Galatians 6:7).*

For the next several years, I would experience a journey that was unfathomable. In other words, I dealt with people and situations that to this very day, I still do not fully comprehend the "why" behind some of things that they participated in against me. For example, there were many times when my workspace was up for discussion. On more than one occasion, it became the topic of the day. What can we do to get her out of there? But it was not until the Lord decided it was time to move that I was moved.

It seemed difficult for some of my colleagues to digest the fact that I occupied the best space in the building. And I might add, it came fully loaded with a touch of Tonia all over the place. It had my personality and carried my spirit. It was where God saw fit to send me, and it was where I stayed until the day of his release. Seven years later, and we all know that seven represents completion in the Bible, and unknown to me at that time, this would truly be the completion of my tenure as student information coordinator (2009–2010 thru 2016–2017). "The steps of a good man are ordered by the Lord: and he delighteth in his way" *(Psalms 37:23).*

Of course, the seven years would not come without many trials. Some that to this very day brings tears to my eyes when I think about them. It was during this season that my mother and grandmother both took ill and ended up in the hospital on the very same day. I recall just like it was yesterday. I was facilitating a training with teachers at one of the middle schools when I received the call. Not knowing the extent of what was actually happening at that time, I completed my task and headed home. Without all of the details, my mother ended up alright, but my grandmother's challenge would go on for many more years until she joined my dad and uncle in heaven in March 2017.

It was also during this season of seven when my dad (Charles T. Wilcox) was diagnosed with lung cancer. For us, this was the challenge of all. Until this point, we had never dealt with a life-altering situation such as this. If we did, I was not aware of it. My dad fought a good fight leaving behind a legacy of endurance that only one who believes in God can carry.

My life changed immediately. I had to find a way to get through this. I just knew that God was not about to take away from me the one thing that meant the most to me. I love the Lord, and I love my daddy, but it is not until this very moment the spirit speaks to me and say, "Perhaps you loved your daddy more than you loved me." I can't imagine that to be the case, but if God said it, I believe it.

For the person reading this book and you're saying or even thinking, "enough is enough," unfortunately, it was not. The season of seven would become more and more grim with details. In November 2014, my closest friend experienced a life-threatening trauma that would shake me up one more time. She was in a head-on collision that caused her to be hospitalized for a long time. My heart hurt so badly I could not even explain it.

"Why was God doing this to me?" I would ask. Why so much pain? What made this situation more difficult than the details itself was I felt as though I had to go through it alone. By this time now, my dad was becoming progressively immobile, unable to do much for himself, and now this. Really, God!

In my spirit right now, I can hear the super saved Christians saying. "I know 'she' is not questioning God." Well, I hate to inform you, but I did. I asked how am I supposed to get through this when two people I was certain of would always be there were no longer there. I didn't want to stress my dad about my friend. and I didn't want to worry my friend about my dad.

"Really, Tonia," the Spirit of God is saying right now. "Really! I was always there. I was the friend you could talk to about your dad, and I was the dad you could talk to about your friend. Really!"

Once again, I can see my steps being ordered by the Lord. God has wanted me to get back to that place in him where I once was. But if we be honest, many people have done exactly what I did. While you may not have had this experience with God, if you reflect on your own life, I am sure you have had this same experience. Just praise God for me that I got it before it was too late!

When your steps are ordered by the Lord, you may think you are in control. Well, let me be the one to tell you that is so not true. All you can do is keep walking knowing that one day you will walk out of it. On December 18, 2014, my dad lost his fight with cancer, and God called him home. A double whammy once again because December 18 is my brother's birthday. I still to this day wonder why God orchestrated his death this way. I'm sure that one day this will be revealed as well.

I want to acknowledge that my dad's brother (Buffie "Donnell" Wilcox) passed away in January 2014. Yes, two brothers in one year! What a blow.

Through all of this darkness, I could not see how God was anywhere near it. But I had to keep moving. I had people watching to see how I was going to take this. Everyone around me knew that my dad was my world. Now, don't get me wrong, I love my mother too, but "Buck" added some value to my life that I cling to to this very day. Yes, I am a self-proclaimed daddy's girl (and I'm sure my five sisters feel the same!).

So as life would have it, in August of 2016, the enemy came with another attack, one that had absolutely no rhyme or reason, in my mind. One month earlier, the school board hired a new superintendent who on the onset seemed to be genuinely interested in the work I had done for the district. One who in one of my team meetings publicly announced his expectation was that the ladies of the team do what I asked them to do. Because I had never felt this level of support, the enemy almost had me.

For once, I was finally beginning to feel that what I did mattered. Someone saw my value and wasn't afraid to display it. Little did I know there was another agenda. One of those hit me in my stomach and made me lose my breath agendas. Not only did the tune to this song change quickly but so did my responsibilities. Suddenly, I had been given another full-time position (interim testing coordinator) in addition to the one I already had. I knew something was not quite right when my cousin who serves another local LEA in this same position texted me, "Congratulations on your new appointment!" Wow, what a way to find out things had changed, and little did I know this would not be the only time I would have this experience before my "freedom" would come.

I must admit, I was excited at first because I thought I was finally going to get what I thought I deserved. Unfortunately, what I thought I deserved is not what God wanted me to have. He used this experience to equip me for the "greater" that was about to happen in my life. Without any assistance (the first time ever for an employee who managed dual full-time positions) to my knowledge, I single-handedly managed the student information system and the testing data with minimal errors. And I must add, this was done without an administrative assistant and without any additional pay.

Right now, I can hear someone in my spirit saying that would not have been me. I would not have done all of that work for nothing. Well, maybe you would not have, but when your steps are ordered by the Lord, you don't have a choice. If you are going to complete the assignment and move to the next level, you will do all of the work.

As the school year went on, it would not be drama-free. First, I was accused of telling something that had been discussed in a leadership meeting. Anyone who knows me knows I do not engage in gossip. If I did, do you really think God would have allowed me to stay in the "place of refuge" for others for as long as he did? Really, Satan!

So just as the enemy would have it, I was removed from the team. But get this, the enemy was not bad enough to face me with this decision himself, but instead, he sent his assistant. That's just like the devil to throw the rock and hide his hand. But *John 8:7* reminds us, "So when they continued asking him, he lifted up himself, and said unto them, He that is without sin among you, let him first cast a stone at her."

For me this was a relief. I am one who does not like to waste the time that God has given me. It is a fact if I waste food, I can get some back. If I waste money, I can get some back. If I waste God's time, I can't get it back. With this being said and after being dismissed from the team, the enemy did not know he was setting me up to excel. How you may ask? It was then I engrossed myself into the two programs I had been assigned to manage and became more determined than ever to prove God's word true. "But as *for* you, ye thought *evil* against me; but God *meant it* unto good, to bring to pass, as *it* is this day, to save much people alive" *(Genesis 50:20)*. And so he did!

Before I bring this season of seven to a close, let me remind you. While the main focus of this season seemed to have been centered around work, family, and friends, don't get it confused. The enemy takes a seat with you every Sunday you show up for church. And may I add, not just on Sunday.

I remember so vividly, as if it just happened.

I was in service one night waiting to hear an awesome word from renowned author, Cindy Trimm, when I was informed that I had another sister who was interested in meeting me. Remind you, I was forty-seven years old at that time. A sister, really!

The informants were so adamant about sharing this information they didn't just stop here. They went on to add that my "biological father" had another daughter and son. As for the son, I know him, but as for the daughter, I am only familiar with that situation, and to be honest, it doesn't add nor take away any value from my life.

So for those of you who know me well, you can picture me "looking like I look" and saying, "OK, and—"

What did this have to do with anything? At this point, I am really starting to feel some type of way. Why on earth would God allow these people to bring this to me in this place at this time? Really, God, are you serious?

What was this supposed to mean? Everyone is well, OK. I began to share this with people in my inner circle, and no one could believe this had happened. Not that they questioned whether or not I was telling the truth but the mere fact of how and where it happened. Really, who does this in church? And the answer is a resounding, "No one but the enemy!"

It didn't just stop at telling me about the additional siblings; the informants went on to inform me of how well my father had taken care of them and how they were both included in family events. For some reason, it was important for them to let me know how "unimportant" I was in the life of many on that side of my family. But to

God be all the glory for the wonderful things he has done, and to God be the glory for my "daddy" who accepted us and cared for us as his own.

To make matters worse, the enemy was very bold. Not only did he continue to use these individuals to torture me with this information, he spread it on thick. Several services later, I was approached with a handful of pictures of which I honestly had no desire to view. I was approached by a gentleman who wanted to cosign on the fact that my father had another daughter. Again, you can picture me "looking like I look" and saying, "OK, and."

I politely turned the pictures over and respectfully passed them back. This was not my reason for coming to church, although Satan was in his full gear and doing what he does best. Was I angry? Absolutely. Did Satan win? Absolutely not. By the grace of God, I had made it this far, and I was determined not to revisit the place where all the pain began.

I kept going to church, I kept speaking, I kept crying, and I kept praying. And one day, I wasn't angry any more. I shared this story so that you will know in your times of frustration when you are made to feel you have no value. You really don't. You have "added value," and "added value" as defined by dictionary.com is additional benefits of a company's products (you) or services (your talents) in comparison to competing products (the enemy that is assigned to take you out). To God be the glory for the added value in my life.

Season Seven: Completeness!

Let's Talk About "Season of Eight"

Historically and traditionally, when it comes to numbers in the Bible, most people focus on seven. Yes, seven is completion or completeness, but let's talk about eight. Eight is a season of new beginnings. For me, my season eight started in July of 2016 and ended in September of 2017. Yes, you counted right. It was only fifteen months. I don't know why God chose to make this season any shorter than the others had seemed, but I sure was grateful.

As I attempted to pen these words for this season, I couldn't help but research the biblical meaning of fifteen. And as God would have it, it means rest (my Season of Eight), which comes after deliverance, 14 (my Season of Seven). "The steps of a good man are ordered by the Lord: and he delighteth in his way" (Psalms 37:23). God is so awesome!

Don't think by any chance the season of rest is rest as you know it. All it means is the enemy has taken one step back from you to catch his breath and allow God to enlarge your territory. All I'm saying is while you feel some relief, God is added more to your arsenal of testimonies, and the enemy is refueling his tank for the next "attempted attack." Notice I said "attempted attack" because the Bible tells us in *Isaiah 54:17*, "*No weapon* that is formed against thee shall prosper; and every tongue that shall rise against thee in judgment thou shalt condemn. This is the heritage of the servants of the Lord, and their righteousness is of me, saith the Lord."

I recall hearing Bishop Daniel preach a sermon titled "Purpose in the Pain." I did not understand it then, and to be honest, I thought (with my human self) this doesn't even make sense. How can pain have a purpose? Well, if you will allow me to continue with this testimony, I'm sure you will begin to understand better.

Naturally, we look at pain as a bad thing. However, spiritually, pain is a major element of transformation and restoration. It doesn't really make a lot of sense, but it is necessary. For example, if we did not have some form of pain, there are some areas in our life we would never visit. If my heart had not been broken, I would have probably stayed in that relationship.

Further, if I had not experienced deceit from people I trusted and hurt from people who did not even know me, who knows, I may not have ever gotten to a place where I can fully rely on God. I will attest, when God is all you have, it is then when you realize that God is truly all you need. Be encouraged!

For someone reading this book, you don't know it right now, but God is going to do some things in your life that you're not going to understand. It's not meant for us to understand everything; if we did, we would not need God, and all of his promises would have no meaning. God's word is true, and I challenge you to put him to the test and see "won't he do it?"

New beginnings don't always happen the way we want them or even when we want them to. For me, the new beginning was the additional full-time job that was an added responsibility. It gave me opportunities to meet new people and to explore new things. Sure, I was in the same place with the same people, but remember, I was serving the same God.

When this obstacle was thrown my way, I caught hold of it and was determined not to let the devil win. I knew this was not what I initially was supposed to do. I knew it was an assignment for someone else who saw fit to exercise her "power" and pass it on to me. It was not my assigned task or so I thought at that time.

But remember, "The steps of a good man are ordered by the Lord: and he delighteth in his way" *(Psalms 37:23)*. This had to be another trick of the enemy. But what he had forgotten was I knew

31

God, and I knew the promises he had made to me. In *Genesis 50:20* "But as *for* you (Satan), ye thought evil against me (Tonia)"; but God *meant* it unto good, to bring to pass, as it is this day, to save much people alive; and in *Romans 8:28*, "And we (You and I) know that all things work together for good to them (believers of the word) that love God, to them who are the called according to his purpose." Now, if this does not resonate with you, keep reading, and I'm sure it will.

After much frustration and questioning why this was happening, a very dear friend of mine told me, "Tonia, accept this challenge, learn all you can, and keep looking. This experience will help you when you need it even though you don't think so right now." He said, "Own it just like you did the other program. Make them both your personal project, and use it to your advantage."

To me, that was the ultimate joke of the day. Of course, I challenged him on this theory of doctorology.

"Are you serious?" I asked. "You do know they haven't paid me right in six years, for the first full-time job, and you telling me this is going to be OK. Yeah, right."

Little did he know that his words took root in my heart and soul. Yes, I was listening, but I was listening in my usual Tonia has to process it her way first mentality.

This pause is to thank everyone who has imparted words of wisdom, direction, and correction into my life. I know there were times when you thought it fell on a heart that had hardened and ground that was stony. But thanks be to the most high God of all gods, it did not. I was listening. But I must confess, I had to sift through some of that stuff that just did not make sense at the time. I did, however, find that one thing that vexed my spirit heavily, and I began to petition God for his will for my life. It is because of all of you this book has come to fruition. Much love and many blessings to you for being patient with me.

As season eight progressed, so did the challenges. Among all of the additional work I had been given, there was chaos, confusion, lies, false accusations, isolation, deception, and sickness. My three closest friends were no longer part of the team. Without them, I was beginning to feel overworked, overwhelmed, and so over this season.

Fortunately though, God has never taken me into a season that he did not equip and prepare me for. Only this time, it seemed to be a little more than I felt I had strength to bear.

To add to all of this, I was on public display, only I didn't know it. It took one of my longtime friends to help me see the importance of how I carried this load. It was him who informed me that people were watching me. He told me how encouraging it was to see me go through and not give up or give in. He complimented me on how elegantly I carried my cross. Little did he know, I was broken into many pieces on the inside.

My brokenness came from so many different directions I would not have been able to keep up with it, in my own strength. This being said, I feel this is an appropriate place to encourage you to keep pushing even in the midst of the storm. Remember, God's word doesn't lie, and I stand here flat foot and firm to confirm it is true. For I know in my weakness, he giveth power to the faint, and to them that have no might he increaseth strength.

Chaos

The chaos began early in the year. It seemed as though everything around us was crumbling down. The initial onset of the new superintendent in mind seemed as though none of us would survive. Changes started being made based on decisions that came from nowhere. For example, one of my best friends with whom I had worked with since July 2009 was abruptly moved to another location.

There was no reason known to any of us as to why he was moved. This of course did not go well, but it did open the eyes of everyone left behind. My friend began to experience anxiety, panic attacks, and depression. Eventually, the doctor took him out of work. While it was sad to see him go, I was glad God provided a way out for him and he is going to be alright. But remember, I was left behind. Or so I thought.

Confusion

As the year progressed, it did not come without confusion. Confusion was all around. From the top to the bottom, confusion was a part. To be honest, I was so confused, but I didn't really know I was confused. I walked around every day disoriented about the expectations and even more confused about my position. I was the leader of a team but wasn't allowed to lead.

When I finally got to a place of acceptance, I began to see things differently. You see, the chaos and confusion were still all around, but the way I chose to deal with it is what made the difference. Remember, by this time, I had already been removed from the leadership team and was clearly working in isolation. Did this feel good? Absolutely not, but I believe it had to happen to get me to the place that ultimately led to *forgiveness*. "The steps of a good man are ordered by the Lord: and he delighteth in his way" *(Psalms 37:23)*.

Lies

For those of you who do not know, I had a long hard battle with depression. The place was so dark I began to forget who I was and most importantly whose I was. But I will not proceed any further without acknowledging those who played a very active position on what is now known as "Team Tonia."

As I reflect back on this time in my life, I can clearly see how the enemy set things up. I believed it was the enemy, but as I write this paragraph, God is revealing to me it was all part of the master plan. There was no way I would have believed in the state of mind I was in at that time that God had anything to do with what I was experiencing.

I was disgusted with everything that was happening around me. I had been falsely accused of gossip, it had been implied that I had written some anonymous letter (anyone who knows me knows I would have gladly signed "Yours truly, Tonia L. Lashley"), I had been removed from the leadership team without reason, I was dealing with deceit, and this was all on the job.

My personal life was a hot mess too. I had begun hanging out with a wonderful man two years prior. Our paths actually crossed in 2005 for the first time. At that time, he was clearly not anyone I would have thought I would be spending time with. For several reasons, I initially met him when I was going through a breakup, and of course, he was married. I wasn't going to touch that fire because I already knew it would burn *(this may be book number 2, if the Lord says so)!*

Time progressed, and my friend and I became closer. He eventually separated and divorced (yes, I have seen the papers). This gave us an opportunity to pursue our friendship. Like all things new, in the beginning it was exciting, but as time went on, the enemy tried us here too. Without elaborating on the details, I'll just say we are in a much better place, and with God we are progressing.

I would be remissed if I did not take this opportunity to tell you all about him especially since I stated he was not someone I could see myself hanging out with. He is 6'2", dark complexion, bald, educated, highly intelligent, military retired, fun and funny, kind, caring, considerate, an all-around gentleman. He opens doors and pulls out chairs.

My friend played and still does play an active role in my rejuvenation. He has helped me to recognize those things in life that once made me happy. The things I thought were gone have come back to life. He is truly a joy, and together we are pressing forward to the next phase in our lives.

He talks to and walks with the Lord. One of the most beautiful and shocking experiences we have had together was our first dinner. This man, yes this man, took the initiative to publicly bless our meals. Not only did he bless the meal, he asked God to guide and bless or friendship. Okay ladies, this is the one that stole my heart. He did this all while holding my hands. Just thinking about it makes me smile.

He loves people, and people love him. He is as one of my close friends said, "good eye candy," and today I thank God for our friendship and pray for it every day. Trust me, I know the enemy is lurking right now. But he'll have to come through me and my entire team of prayer warriors to get to him.

False accusations

During this season, I was accused of the following: not being friendly, not being a people person, and not helping the ladies on my team. I am not nor have I ever been a busy body in everybody's business. That being said, I'll admit I spent my time in my office. That's what they paid me to do, or so I thought.

As far as not being friendly, I beg to differ, and I pray that there are some people reading this testimony who can and will agree. Being friendly does not mean I have to be your friend. It simply means to be kind, supportive, helpful, and not hostile. In the workplace, to me it means to be cordial, polite, and professional all of which I was.

I don't aim to please man simply because the Bible tells us in *Psalms 146:3,* "Put not your trust in princes, nor in the son of man, in whom there is no help." I will, however, respect those in authority, but never will I bow to anyone but the one true and living God, the God of Abraham, Isaac, and Jacob, the one who died and rose for me. The God who came that I may have abundant life is the only God I will bow to.

Isolation

While in the period of isolation, whether by choice or force, the time was certainly not wasted. I used it to meditate on the word of God and to talk to Tonia. In the school system, there is a nonnegotiable rule that all teachers are expected to adhere to. This is known as a "word wall." A word wall is a learning tool. It is used from primary through high school and is known for its effectiveness in seeing a word and becoming excited about that word.

The word wall is a starting place for students to use when writing in a journal. It introduces new words and reinforces words that are familiar, for the scholar student. But, as for me, I took this to another level.

My pick phrase was, "they said put up a word wall, but they didn't say what kind." Therefore, I created a word wall, but instead of "words," I used "the *word*." Yes, I sure did. I placed scriptures on Post it notes all around my office space. I read them and meditated on them every time I walked in. I was determined to be in it but not a part of it. I was not about to let anything that was not like God resonate in my spirit.

I was determined to not just go through it; I was going to grow through it. I knew in my spirit there was a lesson for me to learn. God didn't let this happen because he wanted to punish me. He let it happen so he could push me. Push me into that place where he gets the glory, and you get *From the Pit to the Palace: A Testimony of Faith, Forgiveness, and Freedom!*

I can hear someone saying right now, "She is such a smart ass."

And I will respond by saying, "I absolutely am."

Smart enough to know that regular words don't work in a demonic setting. Regular words won't expose the real enemy, like the word of God. For he tells us in *Ephesians 6:12*, "For we wrestle not against flesh and blood, but against principalities, against powers, against the rulers of the darkness of this world, against spiritual wickedness in high places."

Deception

In this season, I experienced deception magnified by seven. Why seven, you may ask? That's a very good question. There were seven individuals who I knew were working against me. Somewhere in their minds, they never imagined I knew what was going on. When people do you wrong, they begin to avoid you for fear of being found out. Little do they know, when you walk with God, he will expose them every time.

I knew exactly who the enemy would use, and I knew exactly how he would use them. It's funny now that each one exposed another until they had all been revealed. This was all done without me having to investigate or research anything. All I had to do was ask, and it was given. "Ask, and it shall be given you; seek, and ye shall find; knock, and it shall be opened unto you" (**Matthew 7:7**).

Please allow me to share with you my experience of asking, seeking, and knocking. At this point, one of the Post it notes on my word wall was asking God to change, move, or remove. I wasn't specific with that request, but I did, however, ask God, if it's me, please help me see.

God did not change who I wanted him to change. God didn't move who I wanted him to move. He really did not remove who I wanted him to remove. But God did allow the enemy to place me in a position where I was so miserable that all I could do was trust him for provision each day. I will elaborate on this more in the section titled "The Final Blow."

Sickness

My season eight brought with it sickness. Fortunately it wasn't for me personally. My self-proclaimed "godmother" and my sister were both diagnosed with breast cancer. We had been here before. Recall that my dad had lung cancer. It is my prayer that lessons learned from his battle will be implemented in the process with my sister.

I am praying total healing over her body and that God will show up mightily. That God will use her as a testimony to others who may find themselves in what seems like the ultimate fight for life.

I do, however, stand corrected as the Holy Spirit has just spoken and said, "I was mighty then. You all failed to come together on one accord and acknowledge my power."

For this, God, I publicly repent in the name of Jesus! Whatever I did against you, your word, and your will, please forgive me. Don't let me make that same mistake this time.

One thing I learned throughout this process is when you don't do it right the first time, you will be faced with that same challenge again and again. It is not until a repentant heart takes place when you own and accept your mistakes and begin to do things differently. Yes, repentance is necessary for God to intervene on our behalf. This will be discussed further in the section titled "Forgiveness". Stay tuned.

Frustration

Frustration is defined as the feeling of being upset or annoyed, especially because of inability to change or achieve something. It is a natural feeling and an insult to God. You may ask, how does my frustration insult God? That's a good question. When I look back at my personal experience with frustration, I can see that while I was saying that I love and trust him, I really wasn't.

The Bible tells us in *Jeremiah 29:11*, "For I know the thoughts that I think toward you, saith the Lord, thoughts of peace, and not of evil, to give you an expected end."

But me being who I am, in order for me to trust this, I needed to see some things happen. I was doing everything I thought I was supposed to do: going to church, sharing God's goodness, tithing, and supporting the ministry and the work of the kingdom.

I was a good person. I even helped people I did not care very much for. "It's my job," I would say. I was walking upright and honoring the Ten Commandments. Unfortunately, that was not what God wanted from me. He truly did know the plan for my future *(Jeremiah 29:11)*, which is why he continued to order my steps.

No one wants to admit we have things we are not doing quite right. I had so many people watching me carrying the cross of frustration on my back that I had made a point not to let them see me fail. Doing so, I hurt God for what he wanted was for me to make a point to not fail him.

Upon this revelation, I began to really put God first. I prayed, read, and cried more than I ever had before. God saw the hurt and the pain, and knew I was miserable. He knew I meant well and that I had done nothing to deserve this. He reminded me of how Joseph was placed in the pit by his brothers because of his dreams.

I may not have been in a physical pit, but God knows I had been put in a pit mentally and emotionally. I was so tired of dealing with the same issues of life. God knew I needed to be relieved. Looking back, I can now see how and why my steps were ordered in the way God did. For if he had not taken this route, I would probably be in the same place, with the same people, doing the same things.

Although I was burned out and had truly outgrown my current assignment, I was comfortable. At least I was comfortable with the responsibility I had but very miserable in the environment.

I had gotten to a place where I really didn't know what else to ask God for. Although I never stopped believing God had a plan for my life, I must admit I was beginning to feel angry. People were being moved all around me. Retirements and resignations that brought my friends "double for their trouble," and all I could imagine was "when is God going to do it for me?"

As humans, doubt will slip into our minds, and we will find ourselves sometimes feeling things that are ungodly. My friends were very supportive. They answered every text message I sent. They prayed at every request I made (at least that's what I believe). One very special friend took the time from here Saturday morning and talked to and prayed with me even as she was driving.

By this time, four of my friends were gone, and 6'2" as I often referred to my new friend as had gotten his breakthrough. What was I going to do now? I was left alone in the midst of chaos and confusion. At one point, I felt so desperate. For the life of me, I could not believe how others had gotten out, and I could not even get an interview. This is very frustrating when you told some of them about the positions they applied for and ultimate received.

I continued to press my way through the thick of things. I continued to work as if I was working unto the Lord. *Colossians 3:23–24* reminds us, "And whatsoever ye do, do it heartily, as to the Lord, and not unto men; Knowing that of the Lord ye shall receive the reward of the inheritance: for ye serve the Lord Christ."

This scripture became my everyday mission. I was determined not to let the devil have any of God's glory from my struggle and definitely no glory from my life. Upon this confession, the ultimate happened.

If you will recall, I was voted out of my position in May of 2017. I had to close out two major money-making programs with all of this on my mind. I was feeling angry, overwhelmed, and frustrated. But if you know anything about me, then you know I do my best work when my back is against the wall.

I was walking in the same place with people who knew my fate. No one thought I was worthy enough for the details. It didn't matter because God had it all under control. The enemy thought I was going to crumble under the pressure, and believe me, the pressure had turned up. The enemy thought I was going to give up. Glory be to God, the strength came from out of nowhere, when I least expected it.

Being human, I must admit it was not a good place to be. I was growing weary. But each day I would remind myself that I was shaken but not shattered. I was bruised but not broken. I began to speak life into my own situation. I began to tell those around me there was so much more than this. God is so much bigger and better than this. When I began to publicly acknowledge the presence and power of God, like always, the enemy got mad and attacked me from behind. You know, that's what cowards do. And thus the final blow happened, and my situation changed suddenly.

The Final Blow

"What is the final blow?" I hear someone asking. From July to mid/late August, I went to work every day with no assignment for the new year. According to the streets, I was a candidate for seven different positions. Let's be real, anyone who is qualified for seven different positions is someone who I would definitely like to have on my team.

However, not everyone agreed, and that was alright. One thing I think everyone knows about me is I will never do anything contrary to the law, the policy, and/or the procedure. As I waited for an assignment, my therapist agreed that I should put in writing a request for answers to the questions I had. And so I did.

This is a good place to add. I too had begun to experience stress, anxiety, and panic attacks. I was fortunate enough to have a dear friend to recommend a wonderful therapist. May I add, don't be ashamed to ask for help. No one can do everything. Life can become overwhelming, and sometimes neutral people are better listeners.

It is my opinion this did not go over well. It took about two days after the email was sent to even get an acknowledgment that it had been received. After acknowledgment, it still took several days before the face-to-face conversation with human resources took place, and when it did, it was absolutely comical, in my spirit, for God had already shown me what was about to transpire.

Sitting across the table from the HR director and my immediate supervisor, I could see them visibly uncomfortable. That let me know that what was about to happen had some evil connotation. Anytime you preference a conversation with the words "based on," you have to know something is going to be said that will probably rub you the wrong way.

In this case, the conversation began by acknowledging my expertise in the position that I held for several years. It's OK to stroke me and make me feel good, but my preference is to do so in an area that is not common to me. I know this may sound arrogant to someone, and if it does, I'm sorry. I don't apologize for my confidence for I can do all things through Christ which strengtheneth me *(Philippians 4:13)*.

The enemy really knows how to turn it up. My new assignment would place me in a position I held almost ten years prior, in a building with the one person who caused me so much grief. Yes, this is the same person who accused me of sabotage, harassment, singling her out, sleeping with someone to get the position, and ultimately not providing support to her. Let me remind you, this was no secret. Everyone was aware of the issues and concerns I had with this one situation.

At the meeting, I believe they (HR director and supervisor) were waiting for a reaction. What they did not know was that I had promised God, Bishop, and myself that I was not going to give them one. Please don't misunderstand, this does not mean I did not have one. This only meant I wasn't going to let them see it.

In the meeting, I was given strict directives. If a situation arises with her, I was to report it to the building leader. In other words, that meant, "Tonia, don't you say anything."

I was specifically asked, "Ms. Lashley, do you think you can do it?"

Once again, me being who I am, I said, "I don't understand the question. If you're asking me if I think I can do the job, absolutely."

What the enemy didn't know was the whole time he was talking to me, God was guiding me. I really felt like I had the little man in red (Satan) on one shoulder and the little girl in white (angel) on the other. The struggle was real. I was hearing my self-proclaimed godmother telling me "do the right thing," all the while wanting to reach across the table and slap both of them.

OK, Christians, don't judge what I was feeling at that time. If you haven't had my struggle, you can't say whether my feelings were right or wrong. And even if you have, what's right for me may be wrong for you and vice versa. Let's just be grateful I listened to the little girl in white and kept my flesh under control.

I had always promised my mother, my father, Bishop, my god-mother, and myself that I would never do anything to bring shame to them. I would always do good, act good, and look good. I didn't go against this principle when my dad was living, and I was not about to bring shame on him in his death, especially in this situation. He had taught me so much.

As the conversation progressed, I heard the HR director say, "When I have to come down there, the first question I will ask is, did you report it?"

Honestly, I looked at him and smiled. I said, "On a day I am walking with the Lord, yes I will. But we all know there is no one who walks with the Lord all day every day. With this being said, I will still report it, but let the record show, I'm gonna handle it first."

In hindsight, I could see how the enemy was trying to control me and keep me in bondage. The anticipation of me acting out of character was clear. Keep in mind, if someone says to you "when I" before anything ever happens, they are expecting something to happen. I was not going to give them whatever it was they were after. By now the HR director was very uncomfortable. They were expecting me to act one way, but I chose to act another.

While he was squirming in his seat, God had already placed in my spirit what he was thinking but did not have the courage to ask. So, I politely asked him, "Why are you looking at me like that?" Before I gave him the opportunity to respond, I told him I already knew the answer.

The spirit of God had revealed to me that he was thinking I hated this person. But that could not be further from the truth. The truth was I absolutely hated what had been done to me and the situation I was being put in. But not to worry because I had mastered the skills of being cordial, polite, and professional.

Of course now there were a few choice words I could have used but glory to God our Father for covering my tongue. "The Spirit of the Lord spake by me, and his word was in my tongue" *(2 Samuel 23:2). Amen, and thank you, Jesus!*

Finally, my immediate supervisor spoke up and said the assignment was effective immediately. That's right immediately. If I may summarize this for you in Tonia-nese, go directly to hell, do not pass go, and do not collect $200. Don't be alarmed, I meant to say hell, a place regarded in various religions as a spiritual realm of evil and suffering, often traditionally depicted as a place of perpetual fire beneath the earth where the wicked are punished after death. *Stay tuned for season nine—Freedom!*

> But as for you, ye thought evil against me;
> but God meant it unto good, to bring to pass, as
> it is this day, to save much people alive. *(Genesis
> 50:20)*

Someone is thinking well; she's not dead. And may I say thank you for the clear observation. You're right, it's obvious I am not dead, but at the time of this conversation, I believe the enemy thought he had me. I believe he thought I was going to slip and then they could play the "I got you" card. Glory to God my Father, I am here to say he lost out one more time. Finally, my brethren, "Be strong in the Lord, and in the power of his might" *(Ephesians 6:10)*.

Let me remind you though to be strong in the Lord, "You must put on the whole armor of God, that ye may be able to stand against the wiles of the devil" *(Ephesians 6:11)*. Simply put, you must be able to identify the tricks of the enemy. You have to know when he is present and who he is using.

The only way to clearly identify his assailants is to stay in contact with God. When you do this, it's a guarantee that you will come out on top every time. He will clearly show you faces of the enemy and what you need to do to be able to freely move around him.

Remember that the word of God tells us in *Ephesians 6:12*, "For we *wrestle not against* flesh and blood, but *against* principalities, *against* powers, *against* the rulers of the darkness of this world, *against* spiritual wickedness in high places."

Always remember, the enemy's game does not change. He remains constant. "He (the thief) cometh not, but for to *steal, and* to *kill, and* to *destroy" (John 10:10a)*. "However, he will every now and then add some new players to his team. But don't be discouraged, just remember I am (God) come that they might have life, *and* that they might have it more abundantly" *(John 10:10b).*

The beauty of walking in covenant with God is that he will never leave you and he will never forsake you *(Hebrews 13:5).* Let me be totally honest and transparent before you right now. Although I knew that God was with me and that his promises are true, there were times when I felt as though he had left. I felt that God was watching me be tortured and had decided he wasn't going to do anything about it.

It took everything I had inside of me to make it from day-to-day. It was on tough days I had to rely on my *word* wall just to get through the daunting hours. It's one thing to go through a situation when you know why but how many can truly hold on when there is no clear reason why.

It's difficult to hold true to God's promise *(Romans 8:28),* and we know that all things work together for good to them that love God, to them who are the called according to his purpose, when everything around you has turned upside down. OK, so I was called, and I thought he said he loved me. So what's really going on?

We have to get to that place where we rely on what I referred to as "stupid faith." This means walking around the building reciting the twenty-third Psalms while people are watching you and probably calling you stupid. "Stupid faith" is knowing that there is something much better than the situation or the circumstance you may be facing. So let them call you stupid. Be stupid if it's going to get you what you need from God.

I can recall being in the building reciting the twenty-third Psalms. Now, I know there are at least twenty key points in this passage of scripture. However, I kept getting hung up on "yea though I walk through the valley of the shadow of death, I will fear no evil." Unfortunately, I was hanging to the wrong part of the message.

"The valley of the shadow of death, I will fear no evil" was what I was holding God responsible for. I thought God understood where I was. I thought God knew this environment was a low area (valley) in my life. He knew it was dark and destructive. I thought God was tripping. He saw me struggling, but he took his time coming to see about me. If you're honest, many of you have felt the same.

Well, let me help you so that you don't feel so bad. It's alright to visit this place of frustration, but I don't advise you to stay too long. Staying too long can cause you to miss the true assignment God has for you. Just know that God was not blind and he saw, heard, and felt everything I did.

It wasn't God who was tripping, it was me. He needed me to be in a certain place before he would open the door. God knew all along what I needed and had to do to move forward. Remember what his word says in *Psalms 37: 23*, "The steps of a good man are ordered by the Lord: and he delighteth in his way."

God did not have the issue; I did. I was so focused on identifying the wickedness and evil in my situation I neglected to focus on the message. Clearly the scripture tells us we walk through the valley of the shadow of death. The key word here is through. This was God's promise to and for me. He distinctly told me what he was going to do for me, instead, I wanted him to get them.

I wanted God to get them so badly that I found myself reciting scriptures out of context for my own benefit. I chose the parts that made me feel good knowing that they were going to "get got" too. I quoted parts of scriptures such as:

> Be not deceived; God is not mocked: for whatsoever a man soweth, that shall he also reap. *(Galatians 6:7)*
>
> Fret not thyself because of evildoers, neither be thou envious against the workers of iniquity.
>
> For they shall soon be cut down like the grass, and wither as the green herb. *(Psalms 37:1–2)*
>
> Dearly beloved, avenge not yourselves, but rather give place unto wrath: for it is written, Vengeance is mine; I will repay, saith the Lord. *(Romans 12:19)*

I know I am not the only one who has done this or felt this way.

I can hear my pastor's voice right now saying, "Super saved Christians get on my nerve."

Bishop, I must say I agree. Everyone has felt this way at some point in some situation in your life. I rebuke the spirit of a lying tongue for whoever that was who said, "Not me," and plead the blood of Jesus over you right now.

Now that I can see clearer, I can see that a big part of my issue was me. I knew in my heart of hearts that I had not done anything wrong to deserve the treatment I was receiving. But when I think about it, neither did Jesus. So if he had to bear the cross, take the lashes, and bore the nails for me, who was I to question why God chose this assignment for me?

I must admit, I did question God. Really, God? They mistreated me. They used me, and you want me to forgive them? Are you serious? Can we talk about this another time 'cause right now I ain't trying to hear this? Yes, I was tripping, but thanks be to God, he allowed me to trip, but he didn't let me fall.

Can you imagine what a time the enemy would have had if I had fallen? Not only would that have been a disgrace to me but to my earthly father, my spiritual father, and, more importantly, my heavenly father. God knew exactly what was happening, and he knew I was well equipped for the battle.

I can remember when I filed a grievance against the administration for discrepancy in salary. So that everyone understands what I had to do, I had to bring to the attention of the administration the differences in assignments and salaries among employees. I had a master's degree with experience working with people whose education and experience was much less but salary was far greater.

This was one of those instances I used the scripture out of context. *Second Timothy 1:7* states, "For God hath not given us the spirit of fear; but of power, and of love, and of a sound mind."

While this was the right scripture to put on a situation like this, it was the wrong intent. Me, scared? Not at all.

Now you have my permission. This is the perfect place to call me a smart ass. Honestly, that's exactly what I was at that time.

If you didn't use your free pass this time, it doesn't come with a rain check.

This process went on for quite some time. It was wrong, and I was determined they were going to make it right. I prayed about it, talked to Bishop about it, and still no move.

Finally one day Bishop told me, "Shug, you may not get anything out of this, but you may have changed some things for future employees."

I remember leaving this meeting thinking Bishop was crazy. I wanted my money just like everyone else. I was working just as hard and felt just as deserving as everyone else. To be honest, I did not understand this one at all. It was clear, and all of the documentation was evidence. Still no move.

We have to remember that not every battle is about us, and not every test is for us. God entrusts assignments to individuals with whom he knows is going to bring him back the glory. He already knows some of us (like me) will have those moments when we start tripping but don't stop trusting.

There is victory in trusting God. I had to embrace my place and trust that God had all things under control. I had to remind myself there were people watching me through this journey. When I accepted this for what it was, I began to minister to myself daily. "The devil won't get any of God's glory."

Many people knew my story, and many people saw my struggle, but only God saw my tears. The one message I have portrayed to everyone is, "It is alright to cry as long as you don't let the enemy see you cry." Tears are only the raindrops added to the sunshine that makes a flower grow.

Even though you will get discouraged, don't give up. Even when you can't feel him, God is there. All he wants is for us to release the burden and let him work it out. "Come unto me, all ye that labour and are heavy laden, and I will give you rest" *(Matthew 11:28).*

Season Eight: New Beginning!

Part II

Forgiveness

Jesus on Forgiveness

Then said Jesus, Father, forgive them; for they know not what they do. And they parted his raiment, and cast lots. *(Luke 23:34)*

⁸ Either what woman having ten pieces of silver, if she lose one piece, doth not light a candle, and sweep the house, and seek diligently till she find it?

⁹ And when she hath found it, she calleth her friends and her neighbours together, saying, Rejoice with me; for I have found the piece which I had lost.

¹⁰ Likewise, I say unto you, there is joy in the presence of the angels of God over one sinner that repenteth. *(Luke 15:8–10)*

Brethren, let every man, wherein he is called, therein abide with God. *(1 Corinthians 7:24)*

⁴ For I know nothing by myself; yet am I not hereby justified: but he that judgeth me is the Lord.

⁵ Therefore judge nothing before the time, until the Lord come, who both will bring to light the hidden things of darkness, and will make manifest the counsels of the hearts: and then shall every man have praise of God. *(1 Corinthians 4:4–5)*

²¹ Then came Peter to him, and said, Lord, how oft shall my brother sin against me, and I forgive him? till seven times?

²² Jesus saith unto him, I say not unto thee, Until seven times: but, Until seventy times seven. *(Matthew 18:21–22)*

Forgiveness

<u>*Merriam-Webster*</u> defines "forgiveness" as to stop feeling anger toward (someone who has done something wrong): to stop blaming (someone): to stop feeling anger about (something): to forgive someone for (something wrong).

When I think about *forgiveness*, and how it plays into my story, I can't help but see how I prolonged my freedom. It was before me all along. As I have stated earlier in this book, there was much pain in my life. It came in many different ways and from many different directions. Pain is something we don't like to talk about especially if it has been infringed upon us.

I had gotten to a place where the pain from the ex was gone. I had met 6'2" dark and chocolate. I was enjoying his friendship. He has this quirky way of making me laugh even when I pretend to be mad. He made me feel like I was something special. He tutored me in trust and thereby was able to gain it from me. I was absolutely impressed by the fact he was putting forth effort to live for Christ.

Now I know someone is saying that's what they all say. And I must agree. I do, however, see a gentleman, one who goes to church, reads the Bible, and helps me understand things if I have a question. He opens doors and pulls out chairs. And yes, ladies, he even takes care of the bill. He grew up a preacher's kid, and, yes, he veered off track for a while. But I am so glad our paths crossed at a time when we were both striving to live right. He holds me accountable, and I hold him accountable. My way of saying thank you to him for being so kind is to strike his ego (This is not meant to be sarcastic). I often tell him how glad I am he was the gold at the end of the rainbow.

For those of you who may not know, a rainbow is an arch of colors formed in the sky in certain circumstances, caused by the refraction and dispersion of the sun's light by rain or other water droplets in the atmosphere. All these mean in my story is that 6'2" was standing there when the colors changed in my life, caused by many changes in circumstances along with the movement in locations.

Six foot two has been a blessing to me, and I want to publicly thank him for the impact he has had on my life. It is strange how we know what has affected us and how it has affected us but never take the time to acknowledge it. I am grateful he had the tenacity to work with me through my tough places. Keep in mind, this was not just about me. I too became strength for him, when he got weak.

Thanks to God, I had arrived at a place of spiritual restoration. Bishop Daniel was a godsend. If it were not for his leadership and his love for people, there would be no story to tell. His role in my life is so important (especially since the death of my dad); it continuously keeps me on my feet. He too holds me accountable for my actions, but he also allows me to be Tonia. I don't have to pretend with him. I don't have to wonder if he understands me. It is crystal clear that he does.

I often tease Bishop about being his fourth child, the child that he nor First Lady Sharon signed up for; however, they have never made me feel anything less than. I pray for them often as I know they keep me lifted.

To be honest, I am glad I experienced church hurt, rejection, and isolation, for if I had not, I would not have these beautiful people in my life. For that I am grateful. I am also grateful for the student who invited me to attend services at their church. It was then restoration began, I just did not know it.

That's just a few examples of how *forgiveness* can bring blessings into your life. But the real reason behind this project is *forgiveness* that I was adamant about not pursuing. I had absolutely no interest in letting go of the hurt and pain that was caused by the attack on my character. Just as the move and final assignment was hard for me to shake, so was the attack on my character.

I remember sharing with my oldest sister how I felt after I was given this assignment. I distinctly told her, "It's time for me to check myself. I believe there is something God is trying to tell me, and I keep missing it. I wouldn't keep being faced with the same spirit if God was pleased with me."

My sister paused as if she was taking a deep breath and said, "Well, I'm glad you see it that way."

At that point, I solicited her prayers that I would get it right this time. To be honest, I was sick of taking the same test repeatedly. Not ever recognizing either I had not prepared for the test or that cheating was not an option. It was my assignment, my test, my grade, and, yes, my reward at the end.

Upon my arrival to the new location, I was angry. Angry at the fact this had happened to me after being straightforward about me having to go there. You see, the enemy tries all he knows how to get you to bow to him. But for me, I refused.

I meant he was not going to get any of God's glory from my story. Just like Joseph (a Bible story we can all relate to), we all have had a pit experience, whether it was spiritual, emotional, mental, or financial. We have all been waiting on something that would be different in our lives. That something would change tremendously changes things as we knew them.

Genesis 41 tells us about Joseph's experiences and his successes. It reminds us of how frustrating things can get but also how blessed the outcome can be, if we don't lose sight of God. Writing this statement takes me back to the sermon I mentioned earlier, "There Is Purpose in the Pain!"

My new assignment was my pit experience. I did not understand why and how this had come to be, but one thing I knew for sure, God was going to see me through. I humbly accepted the assignment knowing all the time I did not plan to stay. I knew there was a master plan, and I knew that God does not lie. There was no way God was going to let me stay here forever.

There was a major transition in my life, my attitude, and my outlook. I recall sitting in the media center when the assistant principal came over and began to share some details of her journey with me. I saw her with my eyes and listened to her with my ears, but it wasn't until God touched my heart that I heard what I needed to hear. God had used her to make all that noise around me so that he could get my attention long enough to give me my next step. "The steps of a good man are ordered by the Lord: and he delighteth in his way" *(Psalms 37:23)*. Amen!

At this point, I knew exactly what I had to do. Contrary to what people may think, I always try to do things decent and in order, according to the word of God. I asked the assistant principal to go with me to the office; I needed to confront the issue. Please don't misunderstand, I was not scared. I simply wanted to make sure there was a witness to the conversation. Keep in mind, without knowledge (or so I was told), we were both moved at the same time.

The enemy knows how to really do it. I had dealt with this situation and this individual for many years. I had fought this fight a long time with no resolve. I was tired. If I was going to live, if I was going to grow, I had no choice but to LIG (let it go). Surprisingly to me, the conversation went well. I was able to release the hurt, the pain, and the anger. But most importantly, I was able to relieve myself of the burden that had held me in this place for so long.

This is a good place to caution you about the strategy of the enemy. He or she may never acknowledge wrong in a situation, but it's not about them. Forgiveness is about you. It's about your God and your life.

Be very careful, the enemy may try to lure you back into the game of deceit. Don't let him. At the conclusion of my conversation, the enemy stated, "I'm so glad you did this. Now maybe we can be friends."

Silly me, I was like, *Hold up, wait a minute.*

I can hear someone in my spirit right now saying, "Wow."

Yes, this is a fact. In hindsight, it's kind of funny; however, at the time, it was not. I kindly said, "Thank you, but I'm not interested in being friends. I simply wanted to create an atmosphere for success. We have to be here together, and we have to make this work."

This is not about being the bigger person, and it's not about being right or wrong; it's simply about being forgiven and walking in freedom. I needed God to forgive me for thinking I was above his correction. While I know in my heart I had done nothing to create this environment of discord, I was responsible for my actions. I was responsible for how I handled it, and, therefore, God was not going to elevate me until I got it right with her.

Interestingly enough, I had a very dear friend remind me continuously that this individual would be the one who pushes me into my destiny. He reminded me on several occasions of *(Psalms 110:1)*, "The Lord said unto my Lord, Sit thou at my right hand, until I make thine enemies thy footstool." Let's be honest, when you know who did it, what they did, how they did it, and how long they did it to you, who wants to sit. Sitting means I had to wait, and waiting meant I had no control. This had been an ongoing struggle.

Chapter 7 of Matthew tells us, "Judge not, that ye be not judged. For with what judgment ye judge, ye shall be judged: and with what measure ye mete, it shall be measured to you again. And why beholdest thou the mote that is in thy brother's eye, but considerest not the beam that is in thine own eye?" So for you who may be judging me right now, stop tripping.

"For all have sinned, and come short of the glory of God" *(Romans 3:23)*. Yep, all means you too. But that does not mean we can't get it right. Doing so is not the easiest task to complete because it means you have to take a look at you. It means you have to identify and acknowledge your own shortcomings. Notice the word shortcomings is plural. What that simply means is even after we get one thing right, there is always another we need to work on. Yes, I said we, so that includes me!

Believe this or not, God used the mouth of the enemy to acknowledge how close my breakthrough and elevation was.

He used her to say these words, "Oh, Ms. Lashley, by doing this, God just elevated you to another level. You don't know what this just did for you."

To be honest, I heard the words that came out of her mouth, but I could only hear my friend's voice ringing in my ears. "She is your footstool."

Sit thou at my right hand, until I make thine enemies thy footstool. *(Psalms 110:1)*

It is amazing what *forgiveness* will do. *Forgiveness* is the key to unlocking doors that other things may not. Believe this or not, we get so hung up on the things that others have done to us that we forget the things we have done to others. Just as sure as someone is guilty of hurting you, you are equally guilty of hurting someone as well. Don't be in denial, I felt the same way to. Please hear me when I tell you this. You have been wrong, you have done wrong, and you are still wrong if you have not asked for *forgiveness*.

If you will allow me, let me educate you a little on *forgiveness*. It's not easy, but it is necessary. *Unforgiveness* is high stakes pride, and high stakes pride can have long-term effects on you and your life. *James 4:6* tells us, "But he giveth more grace. Wherefore he saith, God resisteth the proud, but giveth grace unto the humble."

Maybe you don't know what proud means. Simply put it, is arrogance, and as you can see, God resisteth (opposes) the proud. Now let me ask you a question. Would you rather be humble and receive grace, or would you rather stay proud and be opposed? Think about that for a while.

As for me, I didn't think I was being proud. Really, all I could see in this situation is what had happened and what was happening to me. When we can't see beyond our own hurt and pain, we tend to cover it up by overexaggerating our importance. We tend to act and believe that everything we do is right and everything wrong is someone else's fault.

I don't mind being the bearer of bad news. So let me tell you. Everything is not always someone else's fault. As we have all heard many times in life, every story has three sides: my side, your side, and the truth. And the truth is all (yep, that's you *and* me) have sinned and come short of the glory of God *(Romans 3:23)*.

Let me warn you though. *Forgiveness* comes with a price. Recall, Jesus gave his life for us so that we will be forgiven for past, present, and future sins. My question to you is what price are you willing to pay to get into the will of God? It may mean walking away from the one thing that you love and cherish so much. But are you willing to walk?

To get what God has for you could mean doing some things you don't want to do. Everything about God is a choice. He has provided the way of escape, but are you willing to take it? If you let God order your footsteps, you may not understand, and you may not even like it, but trust me when I tell you the outcome will be far more than you would expect or imagine. "Now unto him that is able to do exceeding abundantly above all that we ask or think, according to the power that worketh in us" *(Ephesians 3:20)*. Trust him!

For me, I always knew there was something I had to do, but little did I know it was going to come with so much pain. Why I would have thought anything differently is simply beyond me. Remember, this testimony started with pain. But *Revelations 7:17b* has promised, and God shall wipe away all tears from their eyes.

Don't think of *forgiveness* as a burden, instead, think of it as a blessing. *Colossians 1:14* states, "In whom we have redemption through his blood, even the forgiveness of sins." With this being said, who wouldn't want to forgive. Please don't misunderstand, I know *forgiveness* can be a hard thing to do, but when you look at it from the perspective that it gives you freedom, it may take you a while to get there, but when you do, *forgiveness* is a beautiful thing.

This is one time I think it's alright to be selfish. Forgiveness is about God's promises for you if you keep his command. Remember Galatians 6:7, "Be not deceived; God is not mocked: for whatsoever a man soweth, that shall he also reap."

Not only does *forgiveness* have spiritual benefits, but it has physical benefits as well. *Forgiveness* helps to release anxiety and stress from situations that we have long forgotten the details. All we know is they did it, we are mad, and we have not forgotten it. If someone was to ask you what happened, I can promise you you won't remember. Remember what I said earlier, there are three sides to every story: your side, my side, and the truth.

If I may impart a little wisdom I have learned along the way. Don't stay hung up on things and people who don't have your best interest at heart. Don't spend too much time trying to figure it out. Learn how to identify and acknowledge the signs early. If you be honest, the signs have been there all along, we just neglected to acknowledge them for what they really were. My dad always told us, "When a person shows you who they really are, believe them the first time."

Don't make the same mistake I did, giving people the benefit of the doubt. Nowhere is there such a principle in the Bible, and that is why it takes us so long to get pass what God wants us to get over.

If we obey his word and follow his command to *forgive*, we save ourselves time, hurt, heartache, and unnecessary pain.

Thanks be to God for being a God of restoration.

He is a keeper of his word, and he will do just what he says.

> Now the God of hope fill you with all joy and peace in believing, that ye may abound in hope, through the power of the Holy Ghost. *(Romans 15:13)*
>
> Restore unto me the joy of thy salvation; and uphold me with thy free spirit. *(Psalms 51:12)*
>
> I have been young, and now am old; yet have I not seen the righteous forsaken, nor his seed begging bread. *(Psalms 37:25)*

I can't say this enough. The tricks of the enemy are never changing. But the players on his team are ever changing.

> *The thief cometh not, but for to steal, and to kill, and to destroy: I am come that they might have life, and that they might have it more abundantly. (John 10:10)*

Be careful who you let into your space, face, and place. Please hear me, it's alright to check them out first. In fact, the Bible tells us in 1 John 4:1:

> *Beloved, believe not every spirit, but try the spirits whether they are of God: because many false prophets are gone out into the world.*

Faith plus forgiveness equals freedom. This is an awesome equation. However, I must confess. This equation is almost like an algebraic equation. For me, it was difficult at first, but once I got the hang of it, and clearly understood the concept, it became easier with every problem.

What I have learned is most people struggle in silence. In other words, they really want to do the right thing but are not sure how.

This is why it is so important to find a place where the word of God is going forth and where you can be fed. We are reminded of this in *Hebrews 10:25*: "Not forsaking the assembling of ourselves together, as the manner of some is; but exhorting one another: and so much the more, as ye see the day approaching."

If I may encourage you, there is power in numbers. "For where *two or three* are gathered together in my name, there am I in the midst of them" *(Matthew 18:20)*. By all means, find you a place of worship that speaks to your spirit, one that speaks to where you are right now in life and allow the word of God to resonate in your spirit. I can't promise you you will see an immediate change, but I can promise you that you will see a change. I can promise you if you decrease and allow God to increase your life will never be the same, and I never make a promise I can't keep. With God, all things are possible. "But Jesus beheld them, and said unto them, With men this is impossible; but with God all things are possible" *(Matthew 19:26)*.

PART III

Freedom

Jesus on Freedom

Now the Lord is that Spirit: and where the Spirit of the Lord is, there is liberty. *(2 Corinthians 3:17)*

If the Son therefore shall make you free, ye shall be free indeed. *(John 8:36)*

All things are lawful unto me, but all things are not expedient: all things are lawful for me, but I will not be brought under the power of any. *(1 Corinthians 6:12)*

¹³ For, brethren, ye have been called unto liberty; only use not liberty for an occasion to the flesh, but by love serve one another.

¹⁴ For all the law is fulfilled in one word, even in this; Thou shalt love thy neighbour as thyself. *(Galatians 5:13–14)*

But the scripture hath concluded all under sin, that the promise by faith of Jesus Christ might be given to them that believe. *(Galatians 3:22)*

Stand fast therefore in the liberty wherewith Christ hath made us free, and be not entangled again with the yoke of bondage. *(Galatians 5:1)*

The Spirit of the Lord is upon me, because he hath anointed me to preach the gospel to the poor; he hath sent me to heal the brokenhearted, to preach deliverance to the captives, and recovering of sight to the blind, to set at liberty them that are bruised. *(Luke 4:18)*

This is the part of my story I am most excited about sharing with you. But how could I share the testimony without first sharing the test. God is so good to me, even when I can't see it. I don't deserve it, but he keeps right on blessing me.

Like most of you reading this book, people always tell us what God has done, and that's a great testimony. It's encouraging and exciting, but let's be real, how many times has anyone ever given all of the facts? How can you tell me the end without sharing the beginning and the middle?

God is an awesome God, and everything about him is awesome. While going through, I remember saying to one of my friends, "When this is over, I am going to tell the story of how God brought me from the pit to the palace," and so it is. Don't get discouraged when man walks away from you, instead be encouraged. It's God's opportunity to show himself mighty on your behalf.

As I have mentioned earlier, I was placed in a position where I felt I had been removed from the pot and placed directly on the fire. I did not understand it, and of course, I did not like it. However, I was determined I was not going to miss my blessing this time. I was tired, and I needed rest.

After the conversation in the office that day, I began to just walk in the fact I was not going to be at that place very long.

Many people often said to me, "When are you going to decorate this office? This is so not like you."

My response was always, "I'm not. I did not come here to stay."

Let me tell you a little about the office space. (In an effort to keep peace and not to be in direct contact with the enemy, I chose this office.) Initially when I chose it there was furniture. Unfortunately, when I went to begin my assignment, the furniture had been removed.

I was left with a very small desk that only had room for a computer. I had a two-drawer metal vertical file cabinet that I used to place my printer on. Beside the vertical file cabinet was a two-drawer horizontal cabinet. This one had to be turned backside out because the drawers were bent and would not close.

Creatively, I put the two file cabinets together, and it gave more desk space. When I tell you this was the funniest situation I had been in, I was rolling on the floor laughing. I had a trail of ants that went completely around the circumference of the room. There was no window, and there was only one wall outlet.

The telephone I had been given has taped on the bottom with gray electrical tape. I could not use the handset; therefore, all calls had to be taken on speaker, which meant every time I had a call, I had to get up and close the door so it would not seem as though I was yelling at the person on the other end.

The bulletin boards had been left with black paper and black and white Bordette. How fitting it was for I knew in my heart of hearts this was it for me. Remember, I did not go there to stay. I remember being asked one day again about putting my flavor in the office, and my response was, "This is not my office. I did not come here to stay."

My responses to the office comments reminded me of a sermon Bishop Daniel preached once about having something or someone in a temporary position when it requires a permanent stay. In other words, I was a temporary person sitting in someone else's permanent office. I didn't go there to stay.

I began to settle in. Now for whoever is saying, "I thought she didn't go there to stay," I didn't, I began to settle not in the sense you may be thinking but in that I began to rest in the comfort of a loving God who I knew was not going to let this last much longer. Just as we have all been taught, he did not come when I wanted him to, but he surely was right on time.

If you will recall, I shared with you that I sat idle for almost a month without any assignment for the upcoming school year. I also told you that I do not believe in wasting God's time. With this being said, I began to plant seeds that would soon bring me a harvest that was beyond what I wanted. All I wanted at that time was peace.

The seed was planted approximately three or four months before it began to bear fruit. To be honest, many other seeds were planted that never took root. It reminds me of the story in the Bible about the sower in *Mark 4:4–8*:

> And it came to pass, as he sowed, some fell by the wayside, and the fowls of the air came and devoured it up.
> And some fell on stony ground, where it had not much earth; and immediately it sprang up, because it had no depth of earth:
> But when the sun was up, it was scorched; and because it had no root, it withered away.
> And some fell among thorns, and the thorns grew up, and choked it, and it yielded no fruit.
> And other fell on good ground, and did yield fruit that sprang up and increased; and brought forth, some thirty, and some sixty, and some an hundred.

But just when you think it's over, you look around, and there is that little sprout that says something is about to happen. You see the blooms on the leaves, and you're just waiting for the fruit to come forth. The same holds true when we plant spiritual seeds. Just when you think nothing is going to happen, suddenly God steps in and everything changes.

I was called in for an interview for a position I had applied for months earlier. I can honestly say that God had orchestrated and ordained the entire situation. "The steps of a good man are ordered by the Lord: and he delighteth in his way" *(Psalms 37:23).*

God really knows how to do it. While I was standing in the hall-way waiting to go in the room for this interview, a gentleman with whom I had met approximately four years prior when I interviewed for another position approached me, and we began to talk. When the conversation was over, he had connected me with the head of the business department with whom he had instructed to use me as a part-time adjunct instructor. Look at God, and I thought he had forgotten about that one.

To my delight, the interview went extremely well. It felt like I was at home on my sofa talking to my friends. I did not know it at that time, but I had an out of body experience. To this day, I cannot tell you how that happened so eloquently except to say God was speaking for me. And I am so glad he did.

I remember reading a book once written by Bishop Noel Jones entitled, *God's Gonna Make You Laugh: Understanding God's Timing For Your Life!* At the time I purchased the book, I can't say I fully understood the meaning behind the title nor did I fully understand its content. However, I have since come to a full understanding. The fact that I have triumphed over my trials is evidence that "weeping may endure for a night, but joy cometh in the morning" *(Psalms 30:5b)*.

I walked away with a better understanding that tests and trials will come but they won't stay. Suffering and adversity are meant to make us strong; together they help to prepare us for assignments that we are not otherwise equipped to handle. It is in a season of darkness that we must hold on to God with everything we have. We must not give up because the race is truly not given to the swift nor the strong but to the one who endures to the end.

It had been exactly one week since the interview had taken place. Remember, I am the one who dissected scriptures for my benefit, not realizing I was actually obeying and speaking the word of God. Especially when he says:

> (As it is written, I have made thee a father
> of many nations,) before him whom he believed,
> even God, who quickeneth the dead, and calleth
> those things which be not as though they were.
> *(Romans 4:17)*

Death and life are in the power of the tongue: and they that love it shall eat the fruit thereof. *(Proverbs 18:21)*

As we go through life, we are constantly reminded that faith without works is dead *(James 2:20)*. Yea, a man may say, "Thou hast faith, and I have works: shew me thy faith without thy works, and I will shew thee my faith by my works" *(James 2:18)*.

How convenient I thought as I emailed the HR director at the new location to see if the position I had interviewed for had been filled. Interestingly enough, she responded with one sentence that stated, "I hope to have a final decision by the end of the day on tomorrow." This was on a Thursday. At that point, I typed my resignation, placed it in my bag, and asked God if he would allow me to submit it for the upcoming board meeting (the meeting was scheduled for the upcoming Monday).

On Friday morning, I opened my email, and there it was, the one sentence that would turn the light on in my darkness and provide my exit ticket to *freedom.* The sentence that made the difference between what felt like life and death. I began to thank God immediately for what I was about to embark upon.

I remember saying, "God, I knew you were going to do it. I knew you wouldn't let me down." The one sentence stated, "Ms. Lashley, please give me a call."

Even though my dark season lasted for what seemed like forever, I got discouraged, I got frustrated, and I got angry, but I never stopped believing.

When you hear people talk about having to return a telephone call, most of the time they will say, "I made the dreaded phone call."

Well honey, let me tell you. I did not dread one moment of having to make my phone call. Instead, I was so excited I gave no second thought to what my answer was going to be; I just needed her to hurry up and ask me the question.

You know the goodness of the Lord is hard to keep to yourself. It's especially hard when you have a friend who is awaiting a call as well. I recall telling my friend I had received my call. To be honest, I had never before felt as though I had someone who was genuinely happy that I was finally getting a break. Not just a break but an incredible breakthrough. We began to thank God on my behalf and petition him for her release as well.

You guessed it. Not only did God do it for me. He did it for her too. We received our exit tickets exactly one week, yes, seven days apart. How significant is the number seven?

All weekend, I was dying on the inside trying to keep my secret from getting out. Finally, I broke down and shared the news with my sister and my mother. The look of relief on my mother's face was hurtful. Why? Because I knew for her to see me go through the hurt and pain I had gone through for so long was equally hurtful to her.

Even though she had told me months prior to resign and come home, that we would be alright, I had come too far to let the enemy have this victory. Although I wished she wouldn't, I knew my mother silently worried about my well-being, and I do believe she prayed for me constantly.

This season in my life was pure torture. I was torn between wanting God to use me and wanting to react in the natural. Remember the little man in red, sadly to say, he visited me often. More often than I should have allowed him. But let's be real, when challenges come, it's difficult, nearly impossible, to stay focused on the things of God.

Let me caution you, the very second you let your guard down is the same second the enemy will attack. He comes at the most vulnerable times in our lives and attacks the weakest areas of our lives. I know that God had to be in control of this situation for me to get up every day like a crazy person, go to work, and work with crazy people and not end up crazy myself.

That's not to say I didn't almost go crazy. To be honest, I probably should be. But God decided I needed to stick around for a while. He needed me to write this book because there is so much he needs you to do.

You may ask or think there is nothing about you that God can use. Well, I beg to differ. There is a test, testimony, minister, and ministry in all of us. We just need to get to that place where God is number one in your life on purpose. "But seek ye first the kingdom of God, and his righteousness; and all these things shall be added unto you" *(Matthew 6:33)*.

Once we align ourselves up with God and his word, and let him order our footsteps, we will begin to see things through a different set of lenses. There are no tricks and no gimmicks with God. He doesn't woo you with what could be and walk away. He will never leave you dissatisfied or disappointed.

There is absolutely no way I would write anything in this book that has not been tested and proven foolproof. How would I know it's true if I had not been the fool that tested. I know it's not polite to use that term, and someone has cringed at the sound of it. But if the truth be told, you too have either been a fool, called someone a fool, or made a foolish decision.

This phase in this season was extra hard. There were times when I felt like I was not going to make it. You see, usually in tough times, I had my dad to talk to. He would so graciously let me say what I needed to say, just like I needed to say it, and then he would correct me. I can hear my daddy's voice right now saying, "Now, Nay Nay, you know that's not right."

My dad never judged me for how I felt, instead he would help me to be more rational and weigh out all of the options. He was quiet and humble, but when he told you how to throw that left hook, you were destined to win the battle. I wasn't going to let him down this time. Now, my mother is very quiet and easy going. But she can be a piece of work if she needs to be.

Unlike my daddy, my mother worried. Although I am not a mother biologically, I can imagine she felt my pain. After all, she was my mother. What mother would not feel the hurt and pain of their children and become frustrated when they feel helpless in a situation. Therefore, to see the look of relief on her face was priceless.

As the end of the weekend rolled around, I was eager to turn in my resignation. Remember, it had been prepared for several days. I drove it to the district office and hand delivered it to the human resources administrative assistant, and immediately the detectives took flight. That was something I had been waiting to do for some time. In my heart and mind, I knew God was not going to let me down.

As you can imagine, once the word hit the street, everyone began their personal investigation. It seemed to be a mystery to some that I could be so blessed to leave a job and not have one lined up. Keep in mind, this is information I chose not to share at that time. The reason for that was I knew that God was about to show himself mighty, and I needed the haters and the frienemies to see him in living color.

I kept the details of the new position very close to my chest. Only sharing with a few people because I knew God was getting ready to show off. He was going to leave them standing with their mouth hanging open, drop the mic like Bernie Mac, and walk off the stage.

Some people start feeling some type of way when it's your turn to be blessed. As long as they are living the life of large houses and cars, taking trips, holding prominent positions, and making life-changing decisions, for others it's all good. But just let your turn come around. They begin to see far more green than Oprah Winfrey when she counts her money (if she counts her money).

I have grown used to this behavior in my short time on this earth; therefore, I no longer let it bother me. But also don't let everyone in my business. This position was about to be the funniest joke of the century. God had removed me from the hand of the enemy and placed me in a new place that I refer to as the palace in this book.

My palace experience is not one with luxurious walls and doors or extravagant floors. It does not have servants and doesn't have butlers. My palace experience is no more tangible or physical than was my pit experience. My experiences were both spiritual, and only God had the power to turn it around.

As fate would have it, my new assignment was to serve the students of the two high schools in the same school district that set me on top of the fire. It is my responsibility to guide high school students into creating plans that will help them attain their future goals. Unlike the decision makers, God saw my value, knew I was an asset, and knew I had a lot to offer.

The funny thing about this setup is the same people who did not want me still have to see me. Only this time, they have to look at me from a distance. You may ask how is this so if I am working in the schools? Good question. Although I am in the schools, I am not a school employee. Therefore, they have absolutely no say in the matter. Once again, God took control of the situation and showed them he is the real boss.

As I am writing this right now, I am reminded of the meeting in the HR office when I was asked, "Do you think you can do it?" right before I was transferred out. I can't help but add:

> But seek ye first the kingdom of God, and his righteousness; and all these things shall be added unto you. *(Philippians 4:13)*
>
> But Jesus beheld them, and said unto them, With men this is impossible; but with God all things are possible. *(Matthew 19:26)*
>
> Blessed is the man that walketh not in the counsel of the ungodly, nor standeth in the way of sinners, nor sitteth in the seat of the scornful. *(Psalms 1:1)*
>
> O taste and see that the Lord is good: blessed is the man that trusteth in him. *(Psalms 34:8)*
>
> The steps of a good man are ordered by the Lord: and he delighteth in his way. *(Psalms 37:23)*

Not just that, God saw me worthy enough to bless my finances. Therefore the discrepancy in salary that I had dealt with was resolved once and for all. *Revelation 18:6* states, "Reward her even as she rewarded you, and double unto her double according to her works: in the cup which she hath filled fill to her double." Won't he do it!

So now, I am in my new season. My season of nine. According to www.astrovera.com/bible-religion/190-bible-number-9.html, biblical numerology of number nine is the finality or the judgment. It is generally when at the time of judging a person and his works.

Also, number nine is used to define the perfect movement of God. The biblical number nine is a number of patience. Wow, I could not have said this better myself.

Season of Nine: Finality!

Conclusion

As I bring this journey of *faith, forgiveness, and freedom* to an end, I am most excited to have you take the time to read about my journey. As we know, *freedom* means so many things in so many languages or situations. For me, I found *freedom* in knowing that God had done just what he said. He promised never to leave me and never to forsake me. "Be strong and courageous. Do not be afraid or terrified because of them, for the Lord your God goes with you; he will never leave you nor forsake you" *(Deuteronomy 31:6)*.

Yes, there were times when I felt alone. Times when I felt God had left me in this dreadful situation to fend for myself. I was being attacked in every area of my life, and I could not understand why God would let this happen to me. He reminds me even as I write this sentence that life is about choices, and choices have consequences.

> And if it seem evil unto you to serve the Lord, choose you this day whom ye will serve; whether the gods which your fathers served that were on the other side of the flood, or the gods of the Amorites, in whose land ye dwell: but as for me and my house, we will serve the Lord. *(Joshua 4:15)*

I know and understand how difficult it is to hold fast to God's truth when your way seems hard. The important thing to remember is no matter how big the issue may seem, the God we serve is much bigger. Learn to see life through a spiritual eye instead of a carnal eye. How do you do that, you may ask? It's simple, "Trust in the Lord with all your heart and lean not on your own understanding; in all your ways submit to him, and he will make your paths straight" *(Proverbs 3:5–6).*

As I reflect on my life and how far I have come, I can only attribute my longevity to a God who has been and remains my Jehovah Shammah, the Lord is there. I think we can all say there were many people who started the journey with us, but for some reason, they didn't finish with us. But God was there all the time. How do I know, you might ask? I know because I didn't lose my mind, and I didn't go to jail.

If one person reading this book grasps the importance of holding onto your faith even when it seems like everything in life is working against you, my living has not been in vain. My journey was not for me. It was for me to show you and share with you that life has obstacles, life has trials, but God has the final say. As the songstress so eloquently says, "It ain't over 'til God says it's over."

Make a covenant with God that you will be the person that shakes the enemy at his core. When the morning comes, get up, dress up, and show up and let God do the rest. Then he'll (the enemy) know that you mean business. Stop talking about what you can't do, instead talk about what you can do.

> Death and life are in the power of the tongue: and they that love it shall eat the fruit thereof. *(Proverbs 18:21)*
>
> I can do all things through Christ which strengtheneth me. *(Philippians 4:13)*
>
> But Jesus beheld them, and said unto them, With men this is impossible; but with God all things are possible. *(Matthew 19:26)*

Trust in the Lord with all thine heart; and lean not unto thine own understanding. In all thy ways acknowledge him, and he shall direct thy paths. (*Proverbs 3:5–6*)

About the Author

A somewhat shy, reserved, and independent lady, Tonia is known by many for her kind, compassionate, and loving spirit. Because of her quiet demeanor, she is often mistaken for being selfish, arrogant, and even "stuck-up," when in reality she is a typical introvert.

Introversion is a personality trait that focuses mostly on thought, feelings, and moods from the inside. Unlike someone with an extroverted personality, Tonia does not need to gain external energy to be happy. After spending time in groups, whether large or small, Tonia takes a mental sabbatical and retreats for an opportunity to recharge.

Interestingly enough, Tonia has been accused of "not having a personality." Anyone who knows her knows she does not need the opinion of other people to validate who she is, and she certainly does not need their acceptance to justify whose she is. Tonia gracefully owns her rightful place in the father's kingdom, and this is evident in the way she walks and the way she talks.

And it is confirmed in *Romans 8:16–18*: "The Spirit itself beareth witness with our spirit, that we are the children of God: And if children, then heirs; heirs of God, and joint-heirs with Christ; if so be that we suffer with him, that we may be also glorified together. For I reckon that the sufferings of this present time are not worthy to be compared with the glory which shall be revealed in us."

Tonia is super partial to the color purple. As is defined on http://www.biblestudy.org/bible-study-by-topic/meaning-of-colors-in-the-bible/meaning-of-color-purple.html, purple's rarity in nature and the expense of creating its dye gave it a great deal of prestige. It was the most expensive dye known to the ancient Israelites in the Bible. It was the color of choice for those of noble or royal birth or those who were high-level officials. The words alone in this statement are great descriptors of the very essence of this journey.

At the age of nine, Tonia accepted Christ as her personal Savior, was baptized, and began the journey along difficult territory. It was at this point in her life she realized how "different" she really was and still is. Tonia spends a lot of time reading, resting, and reflecting. No one told her it was going to be easy. However, the Lord did not bring her this far, to leave her.

One of her favorite scriptures is *Galatians 6:7–9*:

Be not deceived; God is not mocked: for whatsoever a man soweth, that shall he also reap."

> For he that soweth to his flesh shall of the flesh reap corruption; but he that soweth to the Spirit shall of the Spirit reap life everlasting.
> And let us not be weary in well doing: for in due season we shall reap, if we faint not.

Currently, she is not married and has no biological children. Tonia does, however, stake claim in the lives of her many nieces and nephews. In addition, she has five sisters and three brothers, one of which has gone home to be with the Lord *(Charles "Tony" Wilcox)*.

As strange as it may sound for someone with an introvert personality, Tonia loves people and likes to help whenever and wherever she can.

*****

Cherish the friend who tells you a harsh truth, wanting ten times more to tell you a loving lie.

—Robert Brault

Nothing but heaven itself is better than
a friend who is really a friend.

—Plautus

The only way to have a friend is to be one.

—Ralph Waldo Emerson